MY MYSTERIOUS WORLD

by

Margaret Mahy

photographs by

David Alexander

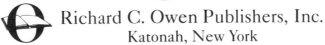

Richard C. Owen Publishers, Inc.
Katonah, New York

Meet the Author titles

Verna Aardema *A Bookworm Who Hatched*

Eve Bunting *Once Upon a Time*

Jean Fritz *Surprising Myself*

Paul Goble *Hau Kola Hello Friend*

Lee Bennett Hopkins *The Writing Bug*

James Howe *Playing with Words*

Margaret Mahy *My Mysterious World*

Karla Kuskin *Thoughts, Pictures, and Words*

Rafe Martin *A Storyteller's Story*

Patricia Polacco *Firetalking*

Cynthia Rylant *Best Wishes*

Jane Yolen *A Letter from Phoenix Farm*

Text copyright © 1995 by Margaret Mahy

Photographs copyright © 1995 by David Alexander

Richard C. Owen Publishers, Inc.

P.O. Box 585

Katonah, New York 10536

Library of Congress Cataloging-in-Publication Data

Mahy , Margaret .
    My mysterious world / by Margaret Mahy ; photographs by David Alexander .
        p .   cm . — (Meet the author)
        ISBN 1-878450-58-1
        1 . Mahy , Margaret — Biography — Juvenile literature . 2 . Authors , New Zealand — 20th century — Biography — Juvenile literature . 3 . Authorship — Juvenile literature . I . Alexander , David , 1956- . II . Title . III . Series : Meet the author (Katonah , N . Y .)
    PR9639 . 3 . M24Z47   1995
    823 '— dc20
    [B]   95-1291
                                                                                  CIP

Editor, Art, and Production Director *Janice Boland*

Editorial/Production Assistant *Peter Ackerman*

Color separations by Leo P. Callahan Inc., Binghamton, NY

Printed in the United States of America

9 8 7 6 5 4 3 2 1

To Alice and Poppy

I live in Governor's Bay, Lyttelton Harbour,
South Island, New Zealand,
in the shell of an old volcano.

Millions of years ago this ring of hills
held fire instead of water.
Millions of years ago this harbor was a volcano.
I have lived here for over twenty-five years,
along with my daughters, Penny and Bridget,
as well as cats, dogs, guinea pigs, rabbits,
and even ponies.

Every morning I scramble out of bed
while it is still dark. I sit for a moment,
blinking and thinking, trying to remember
just where I left off the day before,
and of all the things I have to do this day.
Then I start turning things on...
first the light and then the word processor.
My bedroom is also my working place.
While I work at the word processor,
my black dog, Cello, sleeps on his rug.

Cat sleeps on the fax machine,
where long messages about stories come sighing through,
or on the word processor where it is always warm.

When at last I look up at the windows over my head
and see the sky growing light,
I make my bed and get dressed.

Cello and I go out in the garden.

My daughter Penny lives next door to me,

and her little dog Flynn joins us.

Then off we go, down to the sea.

As I walk in the crater of the old volcano

I talk to myself about the stories I am working on.

After my walk I have my breakfast.
Then I sit back down at the word processor
and go over the previous day's work.
I don't start new work until later in the day.

I used to write everything down in exercise books.
Then I would correct what I had written
over and over again,
until the pages were too messy to read.
Then I would type the story out,
correct it again, mess up the page once more,
and type it out for the second time.
Sometimes I would type stories six or seven times.
Now I use a word processor.
It saves me a lot of time.
But some of the mysteriousness
can go out of a story if I'm not careful.

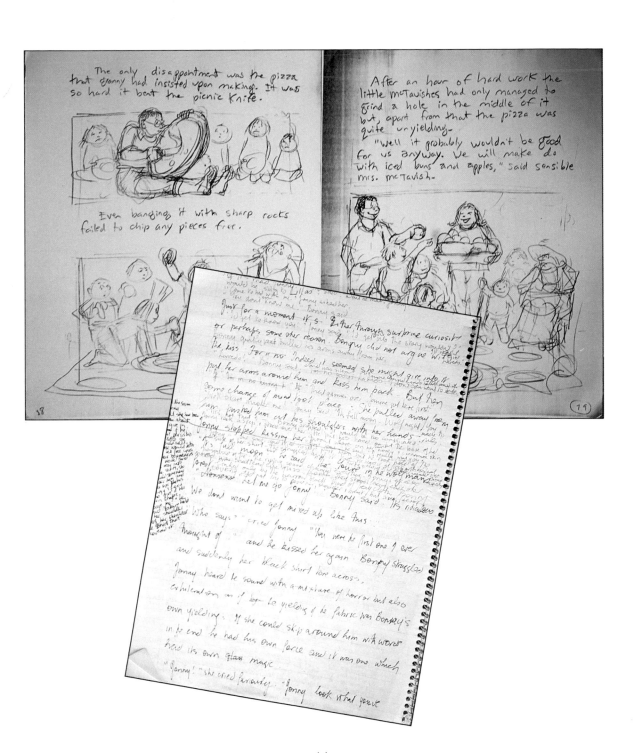

NEW ZEALAND

North Island

Auckland

Whakatane

Cook Strait

Lyttelton

South Island

Stewart Island

Pacific Ocean

I was born on the 21st of March in 1936,
in a town called Whakatane, in the North Island
of New Zealand.

Whakatane is a Maori name.
The Maoris are Polynesian people.
They were living in this country,
which they called Aotearoa,
hundreds of years before the Europeans arrived
in their sailing ships and renamed it New Zealand.
My grandparents left England in 1909 and settled
in Whakatane, where many of my family live to this day.

From the hills of Whakatane,
I used to see the plume of steam
rising from White Island,
a living volcano.
Hills, sea, and volcanoes
were part of my first
view of the world.
Before I could write,
I made up rhymes
and said them aloud
to myself.
When I was seven
I began writing stories
down, and I have been
a writer ever since.

Now I live in the South Island of New Zealand.
Hills, sea, and volcanoes are still a part of my view.
I share a vegetable garden with my daughter Penny,
her husband Robinson, and their two little girls
Alice and Poppy.

We have two big flower gardens
with a long strip of lawn
running between them.
We can run on the lawn or throw
Frisbees for the dogs to chase.

We also have a corner full
of trees and bushes. Alice and I
call it "the forest."

My younger daughter
Bridget lives in Auckland,
the biggest city in
New Zealand.
All five of us own a long,
bare peninsula that sticks
out into the harbor.
We are planting our
peninsula with trees.

I work hard at being a writer.
As well as writing stories,
I have lots and lots of letters to answer,
many of them from school children.
More and more I find letters from children
in the United States in my letter box.
I try to answer all the letters, and I usually
draw pictures on them.

I can draw a cat, a crocodile, a lion, and a gorilla,
and in some letters I draw a picture of my dog.

My writing time is precious,
but I just have to read, too.
I love reading a mixture of things
like mysteries, histories, and
poems. Many schools in New
Zealand have book weeks,
and invite authors to talk to
classes. When I go to school, I
often dress up for fun and put on
a colored wig to disguise myself.
As well as talking about writing,
I draw pictures and tell stories,
sometimes my own, sometimes
other people's.

I write books for many ages.
Some of them are books for little children
who are not going to school yet.
I write books for children who are able to read
themselves, and for young adults as well.
Most of the ideas I get come from things around me.

Once, in a swimming pool, I had an idea for a story
called *The Great White Man-Eating Shark*.
It was about a boy who dressed up as a shark
to frighten people away from a swimming place
so that he could have it all to himself.

I used to work in a library.

Sometimes children would play in the library

until it was time to close.

Then they would want to choose a book.

I wrote a story about this,

but I wrote it about a crocodile not a child.

It is called *A Crocodile in the Library*.

I have written several stories
about that crocodile.
My crocodile stories are partly true.
They come from the memory of stories my father
used to tell me.

The peninsula where we plant trees is the setting
for a book called *Underrunners*, a story for older children.
"Underrunners" is the New Zealand name
for the strange tunnels that sometimes form
in dry, treeless land.

I watch the world closely
in case it shows me
a possible story.
Once, on a car ride
over the hills,
I saw a sign
in a butcher's shop
that said *"Pot-boiling owls."*

It should have said *"Pot-boiling Fowls,"*
but the "F" had dropped off.
The idea of a shop that sold pot boiling owls
suggested a story, but I have not written it yet.

I have a wonderful life.
I have a family I love,

and I live in a strange
and beautiful place.

I like my outside life with the garden, the pets,
the sea, and the hills.

I like my inside life with the bookshelves and the screen of the word processor, where stories come and go like mysterious ghosts.

One of my favorite words is "mysterious."
I enjoy its whispery sound.
It is the word that most truly describes
the world around me:
hills, sky, sea, and volcanoes.

Earthquakes, too, are part of my world,
but that's another story.

Other Books by Margaret Mahy

17 Kings and 42 Elephants; *Baby's Breakfast*; *The Dragon of an Ordinary Family*; *Fantail, Fantail*; *The Crocodile's Christmas Jandals*; *The Bubbling Crocodile*; *Shopping with a Crocodile*; *A Crocodile in the Garden*; *A Lion in the Meadow*; *The Rattlebang Picnic*; *The Seven Chinese Brothers*.

About the Photographer

Rachel Alexander

David Alexander is a photojournalist. He was born in London, the 9th of February, 1956. His parents emigrated to New Zealand when he was five. David met Margaret Mahy in his mid-teens. She rescued him when he made a sail for his canoe and ended up stuck in the mud at Governor's Bay.

Acknowledgments

Photographs on pages 13, 14, and 23 appear courtesy of Margaret Mahy. Original black and white line art on pages 19, 23, and 26 by Margaret Mahy. Illustration by Deirdre Gardiner on page 22 from *A Crocodile in the Library*, by Margaret Mahy, Ready to Read, Learning Media Ltd., Wellington, New Zealand, is reproduced by permission of the Ministry of Education, New Zealand. Illustration on page 21 from *The Great White Man-Eating Shark* by Margaret Mahy, illustrated by Jonathan Allen. Copyright © 1991 by Margaret Mahy; Copyright © 1991 by Jonathan Allen for illustrations. Used by permission of Dial Books for Young Readers, a division of Penguin Books USA Inc. Photograph on page 32 by Rachel Alexander. Map illustration by Janice Boland.